**The Wizard of Spells shows you**

# How to put the Spell in Spellings

Games, Activities and Tricks to amaze your friends!

by **Dr Sue Whiting**

with

**Rick Coleman** and **Deakin Brook**

Published by Filament Publishing Ltd
16, Croydon Road,
Beddington, Croydon
Surrey CR0 4PA

www.filamentpublishing.com
Telephone +44(0)20 8688 2598

The Wizard of Spells shows you
How to put the Spell in Spelling
by Sue Whiting
with illustrations by Rick Coleman
and graphic design by Deakin Brook



ISBN 978-1-910819-45-6



Printed by IngramSpark

# Contents

# Meet the Wizard of Spells

**...who will show you how to do Magic Spellings!**

Inside your brain there's a
**MAGIC SPELLING MEMORY.**

Spelling Champions use their Magic
Spelling Memories to spell words
forwards and backwards. It's your
turn now.

As you read this book and play
the games you will start to use
your own Magic Spelling Memory.
When you've finished the book you
will amaze your friends and surprise
your teachers by doing Magic Spellings.
Before you start, meet my friends...

# Meet Bramble

I'm Bramble, the Wizard's very special cat.

Being a cat I've always been very clever.
Now that the Wizard's taught me his Magic
Spelling secrets, I'm brilliant!

He's asked me to help Charlie and Holly do
Magic Spellings.  Sometimes they're very slow.
I bet you'll be much quicker than them.

# Meet the Brian Cells

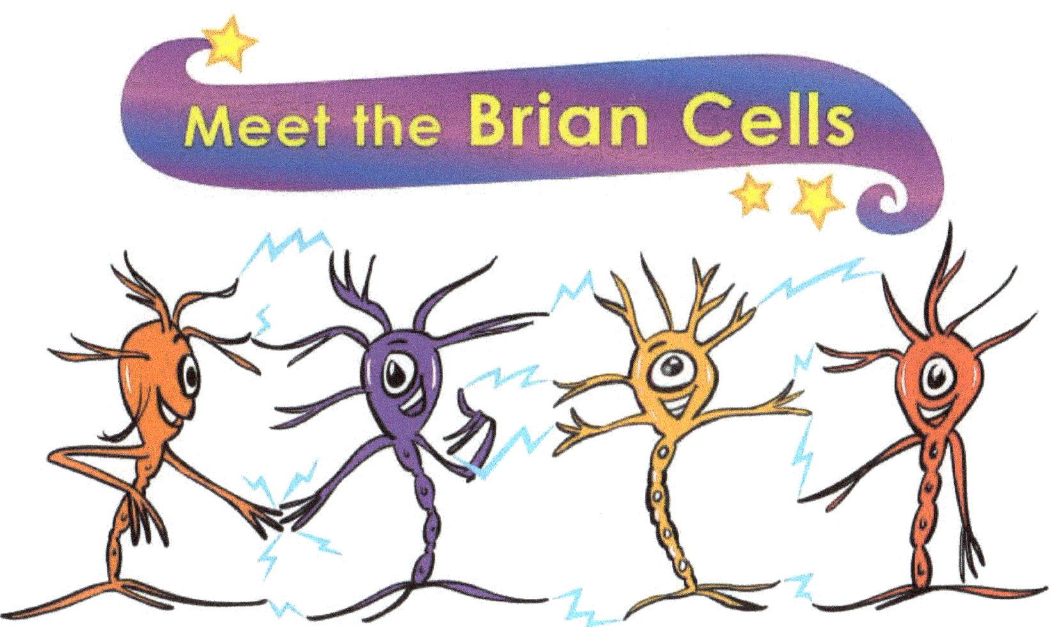

We are The Brian Cells.
Scientists know us as Brain Cells because we live inside your Brain,
but Spellers call us Brian Cells.
When you learn things we join up to make lots of sparks!
WOW ! It's a fantastic feeling!
We love it when you learn new spellings!
Oooooooh all those lovely sparks. That's what we live for.

Then at night, when you're asleep, we're the super cleaners.
1.  We throw away all the rubbish.
2.  We tidy up all the spellings you've learned and put them away
    in safe places so you can find them the next day.
3.  We then give your brain a quick clean, to make lots of room for
    all the new spellings you want to learn.

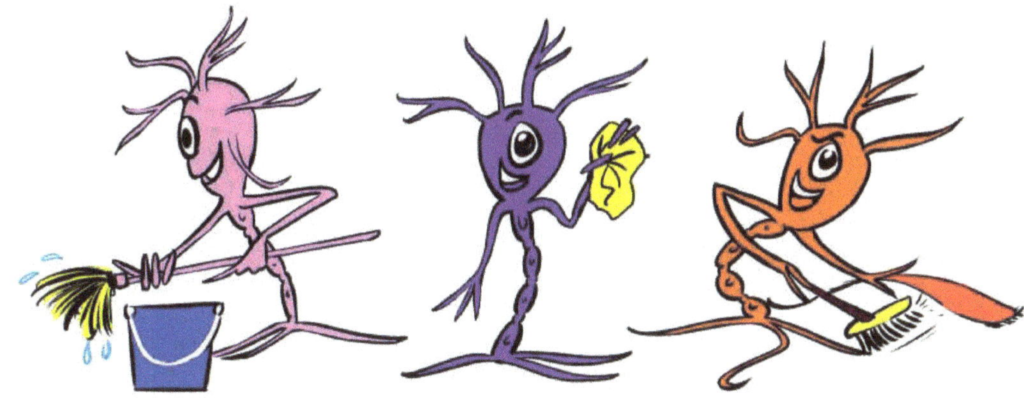

WOOF!  I'm Charlie!
I'm a yellow Labrador and a very happy waggy tailed dog.
The best time of my day is eating my dinner. It doesn't last long enough, though. The next best time is breakfast. That's over too quickly too.
When I'm not eating I love chasing balls and chewing bones.
Bramble's going to help me learn my spellings.
Will you help if I get stuck?
It might mean I can find more food!

WOOF!  I'm Holly!
I'm a brown Labrador and a very happy waggy tailed dog.
Charlie's my best friend.
I love my breakfasts and dinners – and any other food I can find.
I can't spell so sometimes I order the wrong things from the internet.
But guess what... Bramble's going to help me with my spellings. Isn't that cool! I'll soon be able to order all the doggy treats I want.
Yummy!  Yummy!

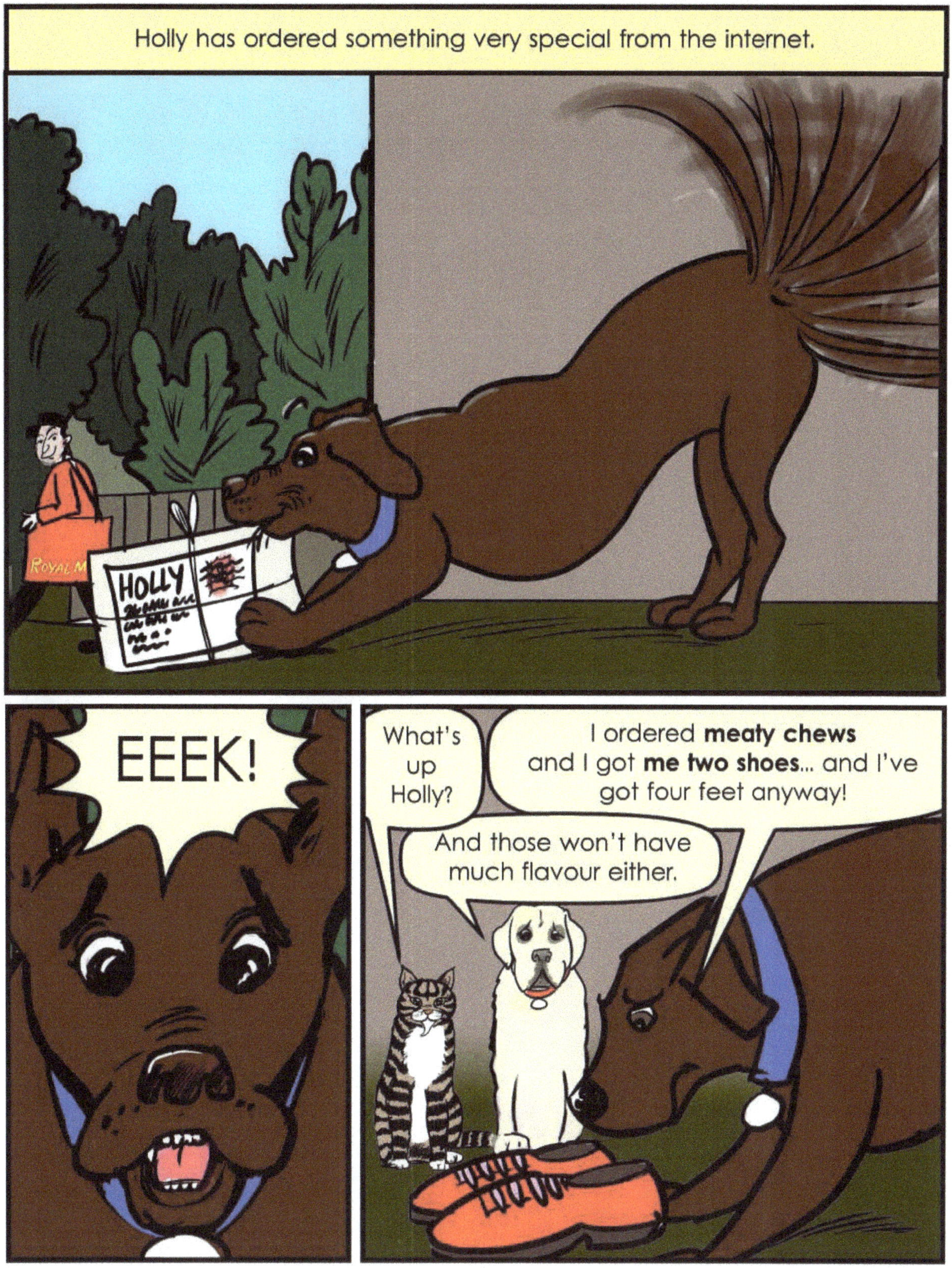

Holly has ordered something very special from the internet.

EEEK!

What's up Holly?
I ordered meaty chews and I got me two shoes... and I've got four feet anyway!
And those won't have much flavour either.

How did that happen?
Ah ha...I bet you typed **me two** instead of **meaty** and **shoes** instead of **chews**.

This mustn't happen again. You must learn how to spell.
But spellings are so hard.

My Magic Spelling way is easy. Shall I show you?
Yes please!

Charlie and Holly really need some help with their spellings. Only the other day Holly thought she'd ordered some delicious Meaty Chews. She was so upset when two shoes arrived instead!

Please will you help Holly and Charlie learn how to spell words? Then they can order all the right things from the internet.

As you read this book you'll learn tricks from Spelling Champions. Every time you get the games and quizzes right you can colour in one bit of Holly's picture on the next page. It's a magic picture (well, I am a Wizard). So once it's complete Holly will finally be able to get what she wants from the internet. But it only works if you play the games and get those puzzles right...

Poor Holly, she's still so unhappy. There's no time to be wasted. Off you go to help her.

# Colouring in

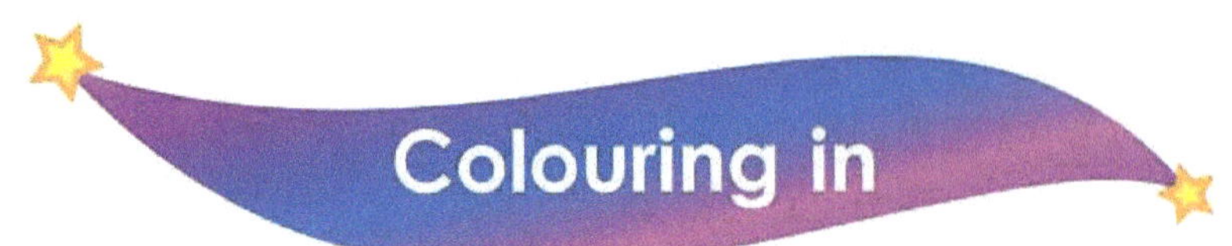

**Page 19**
Colour in
the trees

**Page 26/27**
Colour in
the fence

**Page 34**
Colour in
the package

**Page 35**
Colour in
Holly's collar

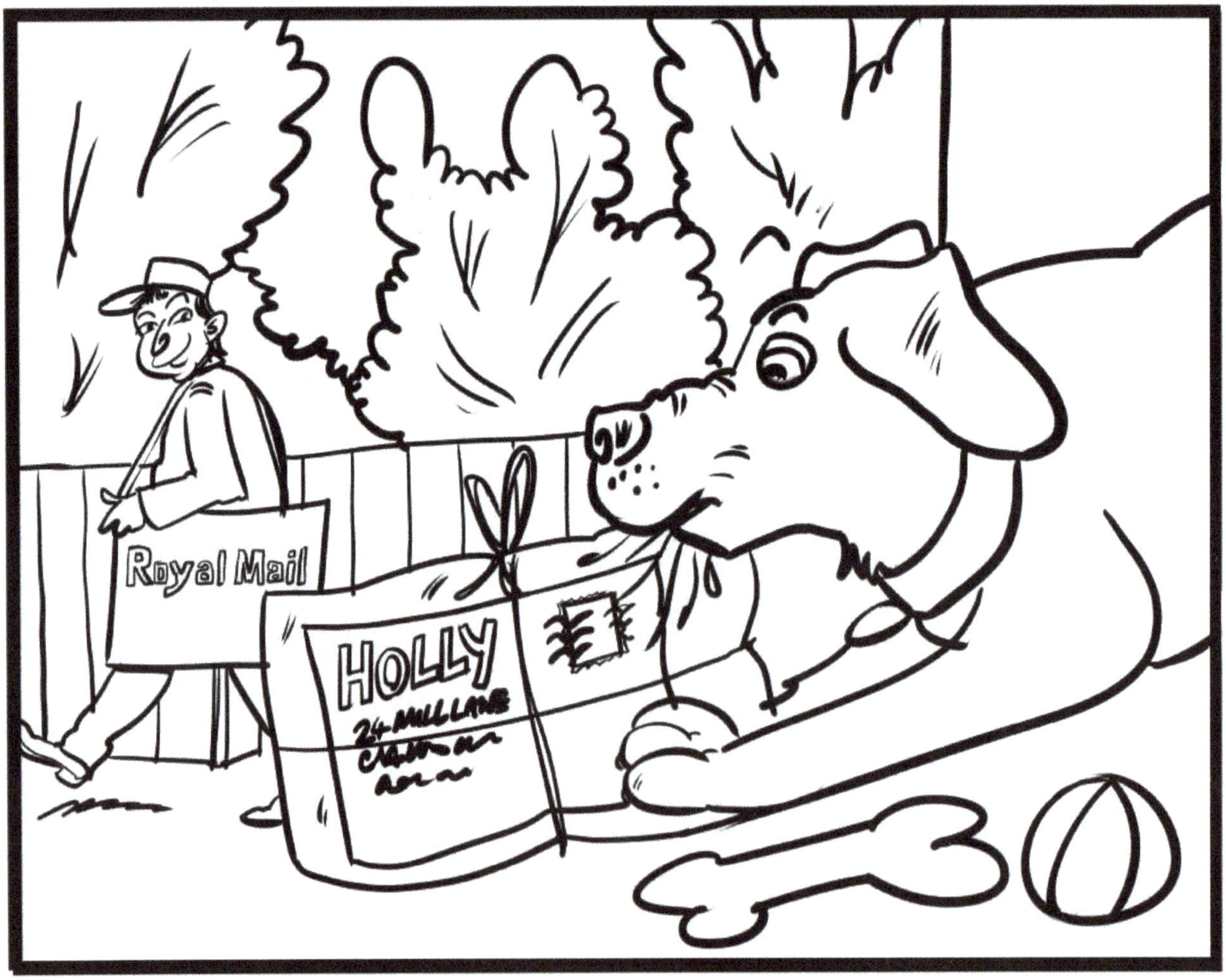


**Page 36**
Colour in
the postman

**Page 39**
Colour in
the grass

**Page 47**
Colour in
Holly's toys

**Page 54**
Colour in
Holly

# The best way to learn how to do anything

# How Spelling Champions do their spellings

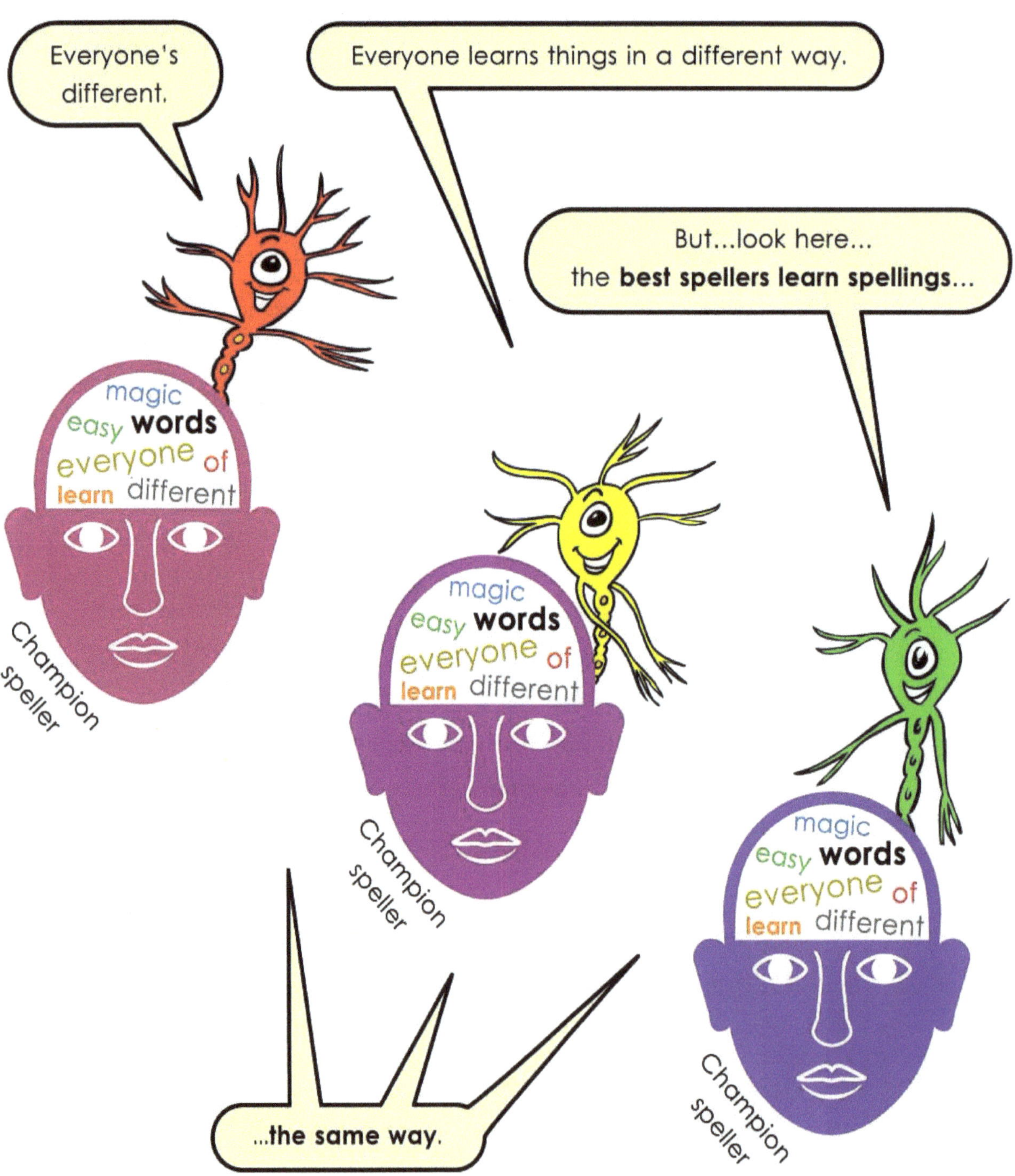

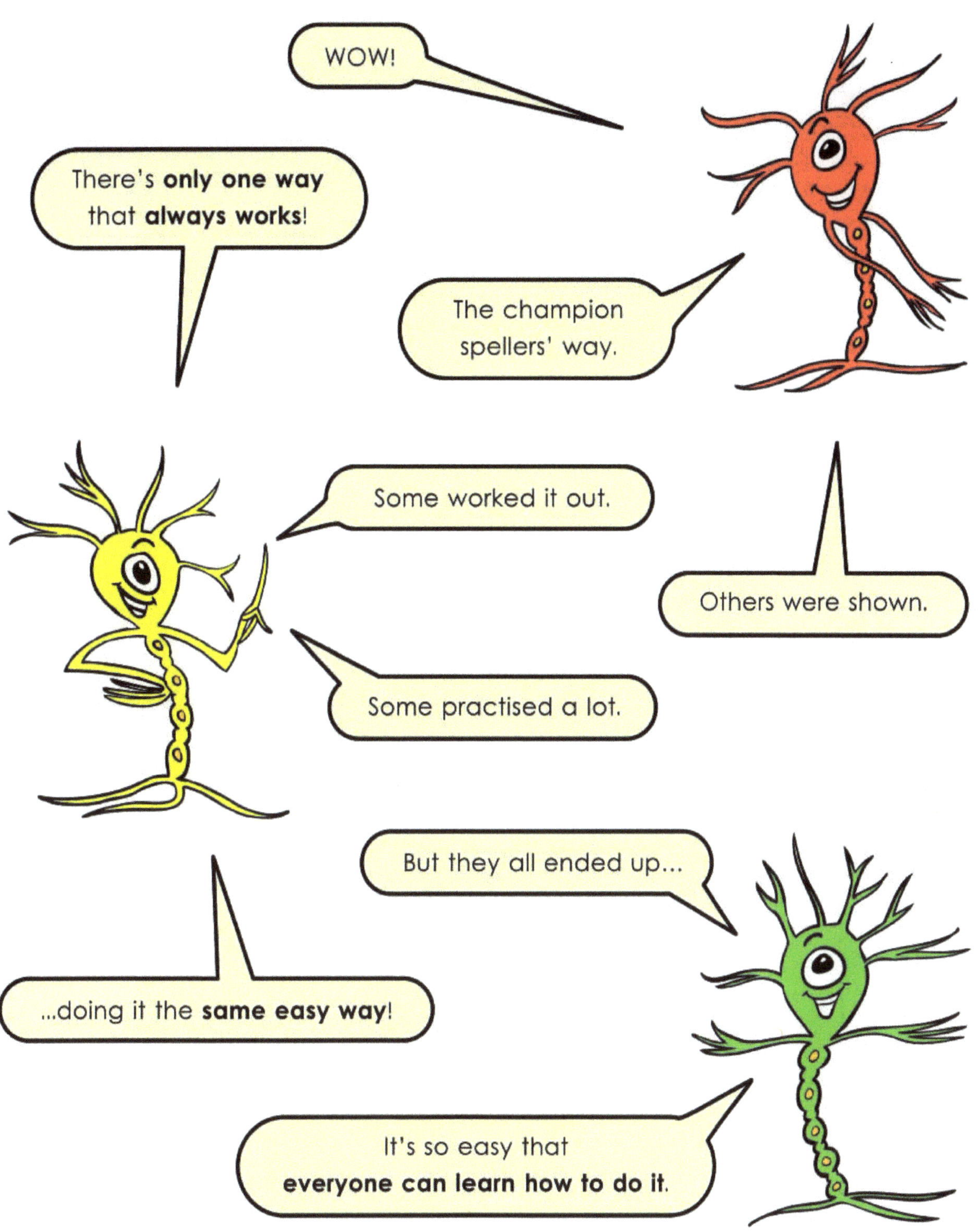

WOW!
There's **only one way** that **always works**!
The champion spellers' way.
Some worked it out.
Others were shown.
Some practised a lot.
But they all ended up...
...doing it the **same easy way**!
It's so easy that **everyone can learn how to do it**.

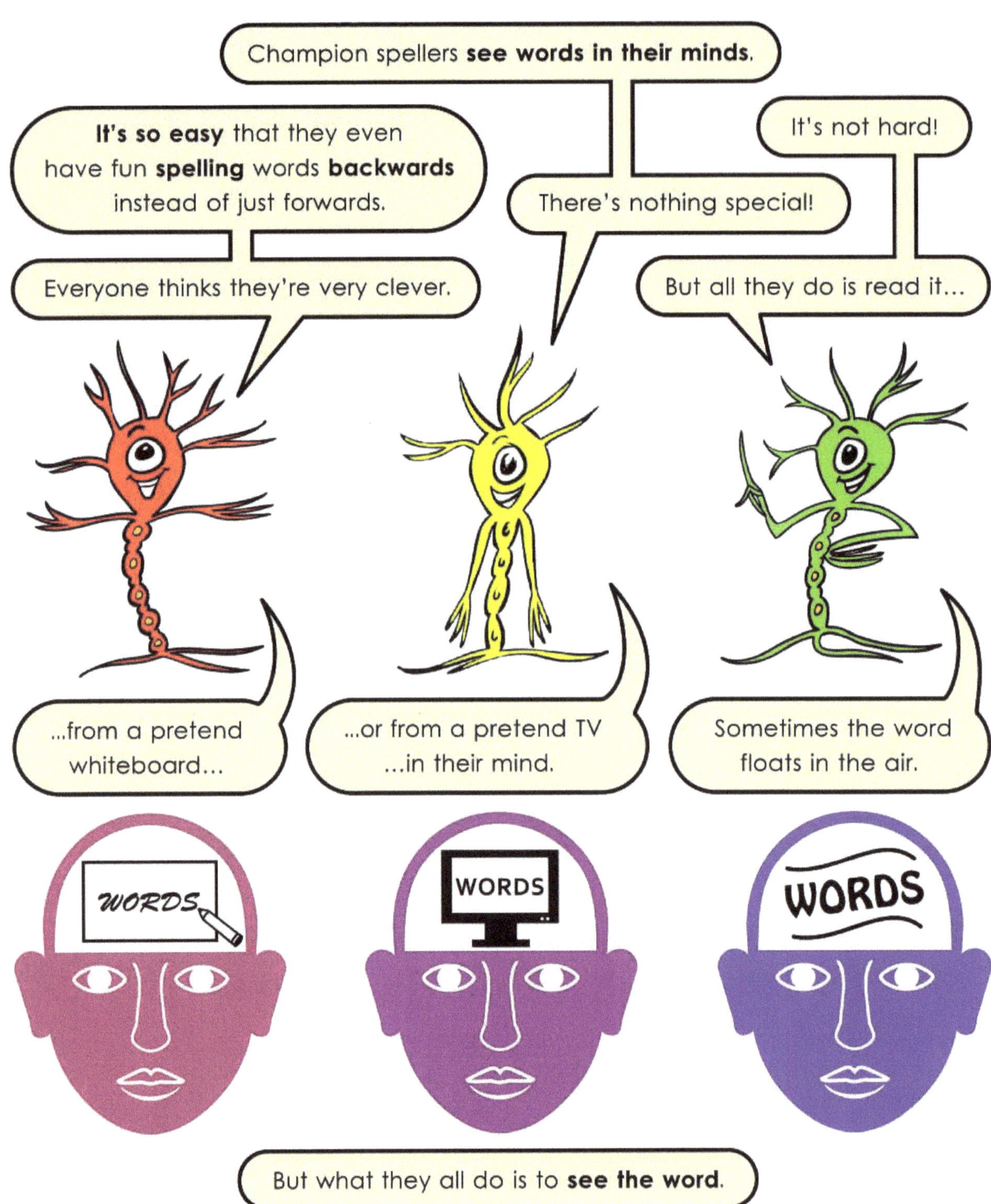

Champion spellers see words in their minds.
It's so easy that they even have fun spelling words backwards instead of just forwards.
There's nothing special!
It's not hard!
Everyone thinks they're very clever.
But all they do is read it...
...from a pretend whiteboard...
...or from a pretend TV ...in their mind.
Sometimes the word floats in the air.
WORDS
WORDS
WORDS
But what they all do is to see the word.

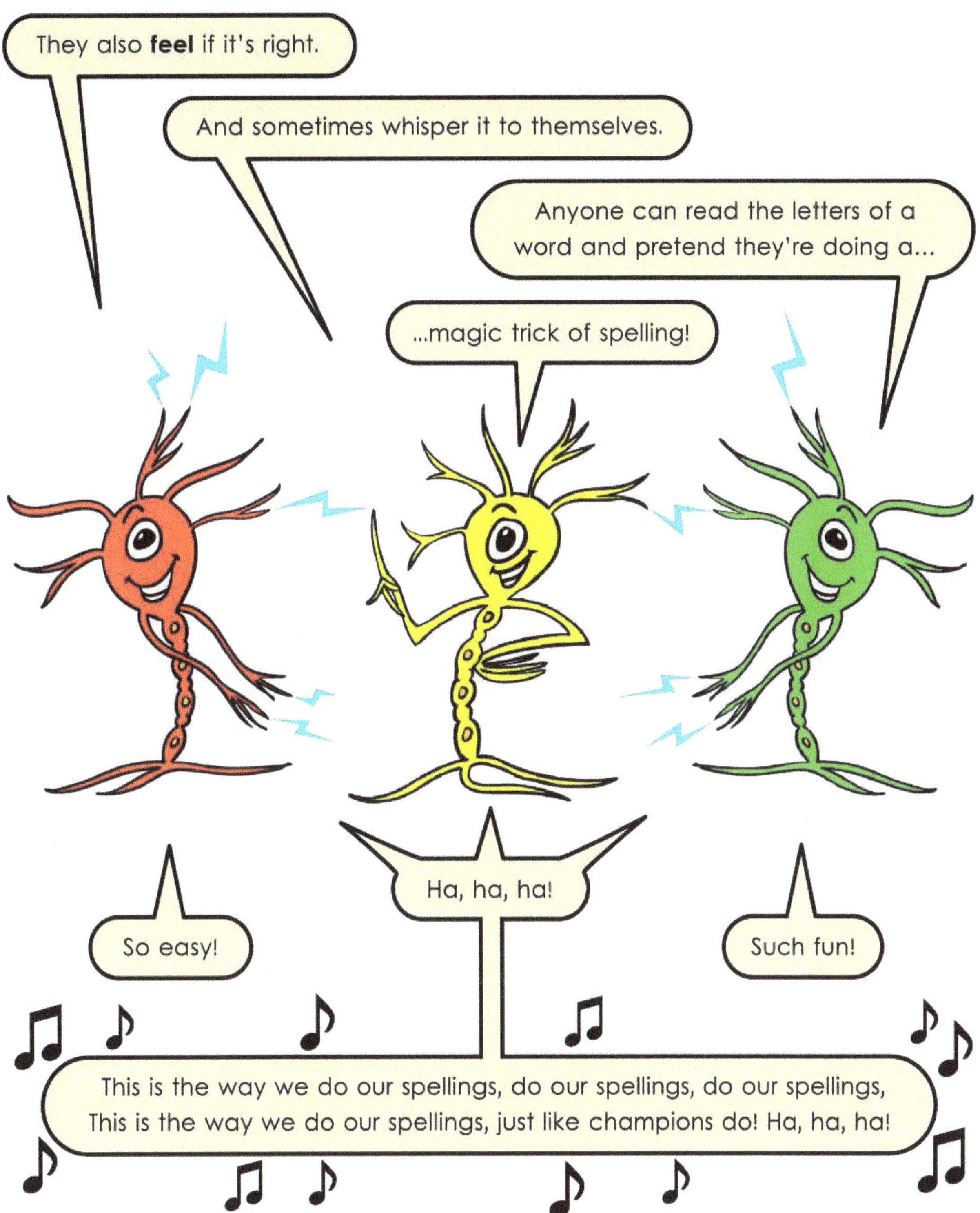

They also **feel** if it's right.
And sometimes whisper it to themselves.
Anyone can read the letters of a word and pretend they're doing a...
...magic trick of spelling!
Ha, ha, ha!
So easy!
Such fun!
This is the way we do our spellings, do our spellings, do our spellings,
This is the way we do our spellings, just like champions do! Ha, ha, ha!

## Magic Spelling Tip

Champion spellers **'see'** the word they're spelling in their mind's eye.

It's SO easy to do!

They think that everyone else does it this way.

They don't even realise this is the biggest secret of all time!

Bramble explains why Spelling Champions 'see' the words in their minds.

How many sounds are there in English?

Sounds?
Well we know the alphabet... let's count it up Holly. A 1, B 2, ...

A long time later...
... Z 26. So 26 letters means 26 sounds.
Duh... I didn't get 26. But you'll be right, Charlie: 26 sounds.

NO! Fooled you! There are far more than 26.
What about sounds like th...ch...sh...ou...ai?
Doh! Another trick question!

How many sounds are there, Bramble?
English has 44 sounds.

Okay. We believe you.

How many ways are there to spell 44 sounds?
44.


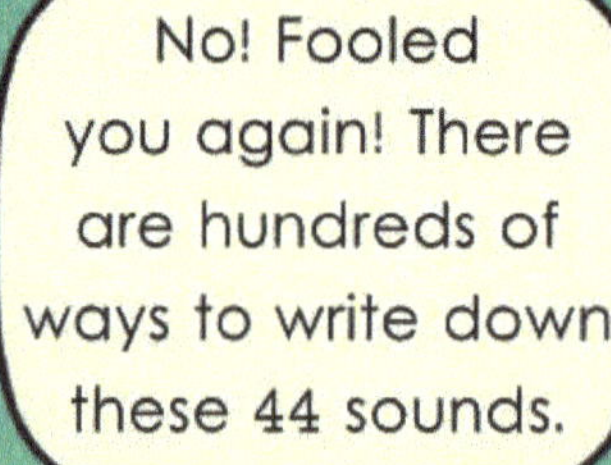

Yes 44. Come on Charlie. I've had enough of sounds and spellings. Let's play ball in the park.
No! Fooled you again! There are hundreds of ways to write down these 44 sounds.
Why?
How?

Do the Word Search on the next page... all the words have the EEE sound– but it's spelled in lots of different ways.

# Wizard's Wordsearch

Find these words in the word search: they all have the sound 'eee' in them.

**be**
**bee**
**beech**
**beach**
**cathedral**
**Charlie**
**cheese**
**debris**
**easy**
**eat**
**Holly**
**key**
**peace**
**people**
**piece**
**pizza**
**police**
**protein**
**quay**
**queen**
**receive**
**see**
**sea**
**secret**
**sweet**
**ski**
**these**
**thief**
**wheeze**

| c | h | a | r | l | i | e | s | e | e | i | k | k | r | r |
|---|---|---|---|---|---|---|---|---|---|---|---|---|---|---|
| d | e | b | r | i | s | i | e | a | t | h | o | l | l | y |
| a | t | h | e | s | e | k | r | r | o | b | e | a | c | h |
| c | a | t | h | e | d | r | a | l | p | o | l | i | c | e |
| a | b | r | s | e | c | r | e | t | q | b | e | e | c | h |
| p | e | o | p | l | e | f | l | o | r | s | q | u | a | y |
| r | s | e | a | c | c | w | h | e | e | z | e | o | h | o |
| r | e | c | e | i | v | e | c | z | w | y | o | l | b | e |
| m | p | r | z | k | j | u | b | e | e | q | g | h | i | i |
| e | s | w | e | e | t | c | e | n | t | h | i | e | f | h |
| p | i | e | c | e | q | w | r | t | a | p | i | z | z | a |
| l | p | r | o | t | e | i | n | a | c | q | s | h | y | m |
| k | r | p | e | a | c | e | c | h | e | e | s | e | w | v |
| u | e | v | q | u | e | e | n | h | v | e | a | s | y | h |
| s | k | i | l | y | n | c | k | e | y | d | e | x | e | s |

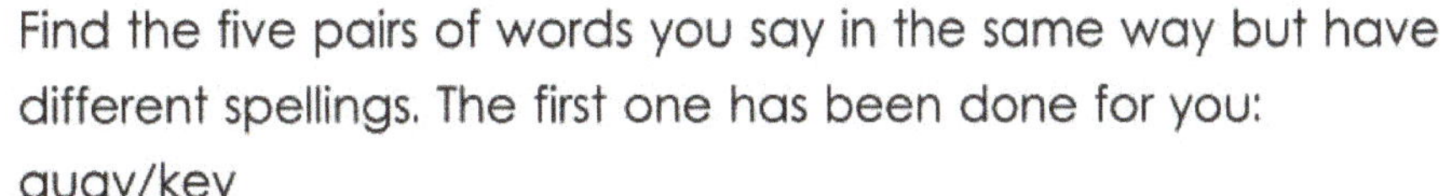

Find the five pairs of words you say in the same way but have different spellings. The first one has been done for you:
quay/key

_______________________________________

_______________________________________

How many different ways can you find to make the sound 'eee'?

_______________________________________

**Check your answers to colour in the next bit of Holly's picture.**

Did you find the 15 ways to spell EEE?
How can you possibly work out which EEE spelling to use when there are so many different ways?
Yes. Even our names have different EEE spellings.

Holly! That's why spellings are hard. I work them all out...
Duh... so hard... too much thinking... and I get them wrong.

It's much easier to take photos of words in your mind.
Cool.

What's the catch?
No catch...no tricks...it works. Just learn to see words in your mind.

click!
click!
Easy
Key
Pizza
click!
Free
click!
click!

A Spelling Champion explains how she does it.

So how do you do it?
It's easy. There's nothing to it. I see the word in front of me.
So all I do is to read out the letters. Dead easy. You can read out letters the teacher has written on the whiteboard, can't you?
Yes.
So what's all the fuss about? It's the same thing. Anyone can learn how to do it.
How can the word be in the front of you?
Well it just is – as soon as I think of spelling it.
Why don't you tell everyone this is how you do it?
I thought everyone 'saw' words. No-one's ever asked me what goes on in my head before.

Go to the next page to read about a champion speller called Alex, who has his own YouTube channel 'The Secret Spell to Spelling'.

# Alex A Lexicon

In class the next day...
Miss! Have you seen Mary Poppins?

Yes. It's good, isn't it?

Well I can spell supercalifragilistic-expialidocious.
WOW!
No way!

I wonder if he can.
I can't even say it.
I can only say it if I sing it.

Off you go. I'll write it down as you say it.

Well done, Alex. Let's give him a big clap.
Supercalifra ilistic
WHOOP!
WHOOP!
CLAP!
CLAP!
CLAP!

But Alex hasn't finished yet...
I'll do it backwards now.
Backwards?
Start at the end with the 's'.

Why does he want to do that?
OK...have a quick go before we do our sums. Turn around so you can't see the board.
gi listicexpialidocious
Be amazing if he can...
Never seen this before...

I'll point to letters as you say them. Do you want the first one?
Supercalifragilisticexpialidocious
WOW!
No thanks.  suo… x…f…epus!
That is magic!
He makes it look so easy!
I can see the whole word in my mind
Gasp!

Excellent! Perhaps one day you'll teach us how to do it.

That night when Alex got home he was very busy…
I'll split Saturday into 3 bits… Sat-ur-day…
…that they write on 3 different coloured cards…

…that they hold up to take photos in their minds…
CLICK! CLICK! CLICK!
SAT UR DAY

…then they close their eyes to check they can see it in their minds…
SAT UR DAY

Yep. That'll work brilliantly. I'll write a book called 'The Secret Spell to Spelling' to help everyone!

*A lexicon is a type of dictionary.*

#  Quiz

Write the letter **T** for true or **F** for false.

Champion spellers:

...... **see words in their minds.**

...... **can spell out all the letters of words they've learned.**

...... **do spelling tests using pens held between their toes.**

...... **just read out the letters or words they see in front of them.**

...... **can spell out words backwards as well as forwards (they start at the end).**

...... **think everyone spells their way.**

...... **always stand on their heads to do spelling tests.**

**Colour in the next bit of Holly's picture before you turn over the page to learn some more magic spelling secrets!**

# More Magic Spelling Tips

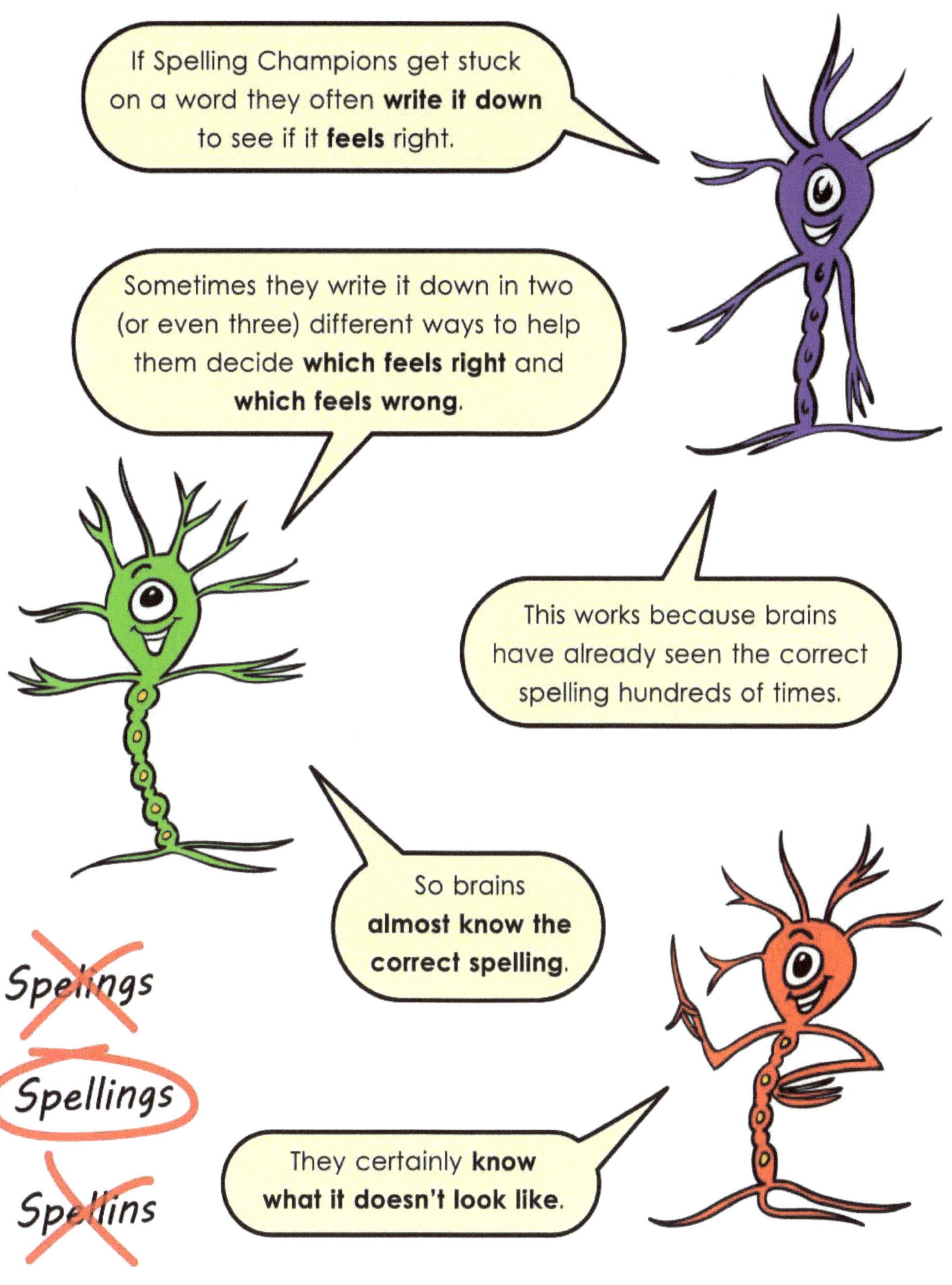

If Spelling Champions get stuck on a word they often **write it down** to see if it **feels** right.
Sometimes they write it down in two (or even three) different ways to help them decide **which feels right** and **which feels wrong**.
This works because brains have already seen the correct spelling hundreds of times.
So brains **almost know the correct spelling**.
They certainly **know what it doesn't look like**.
Spellings
Spellings
Spellins

Magic Spelling Tip
Spelling Champions look
at all the letters.

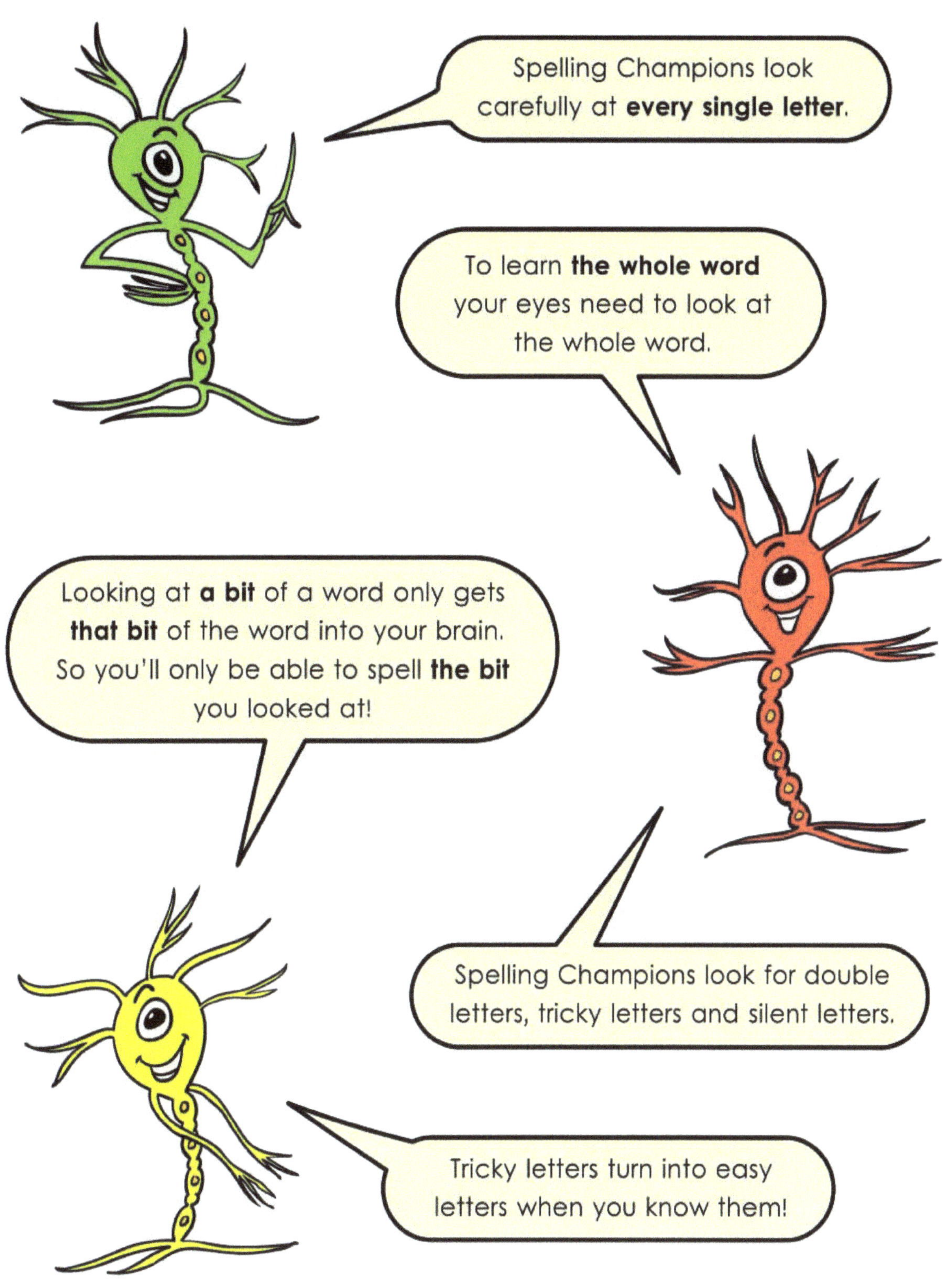

Spelling Champions look carefully at every single letter.
To learn the whole word your eyes need to look at the whole word.
Looking at a bit of a word only gets that bit of the word into your brain. So you'll only be able to spell the bit you looked at!
Spelling Champions look for double letters, tricky letters and silent letters.
Tricky letters turn into easy letters when you know them!

Magic Spelling Tip

Spelling Champions **look for things they already know**. They **see words in words** and **easy chunks to make it much easier to spell things**.

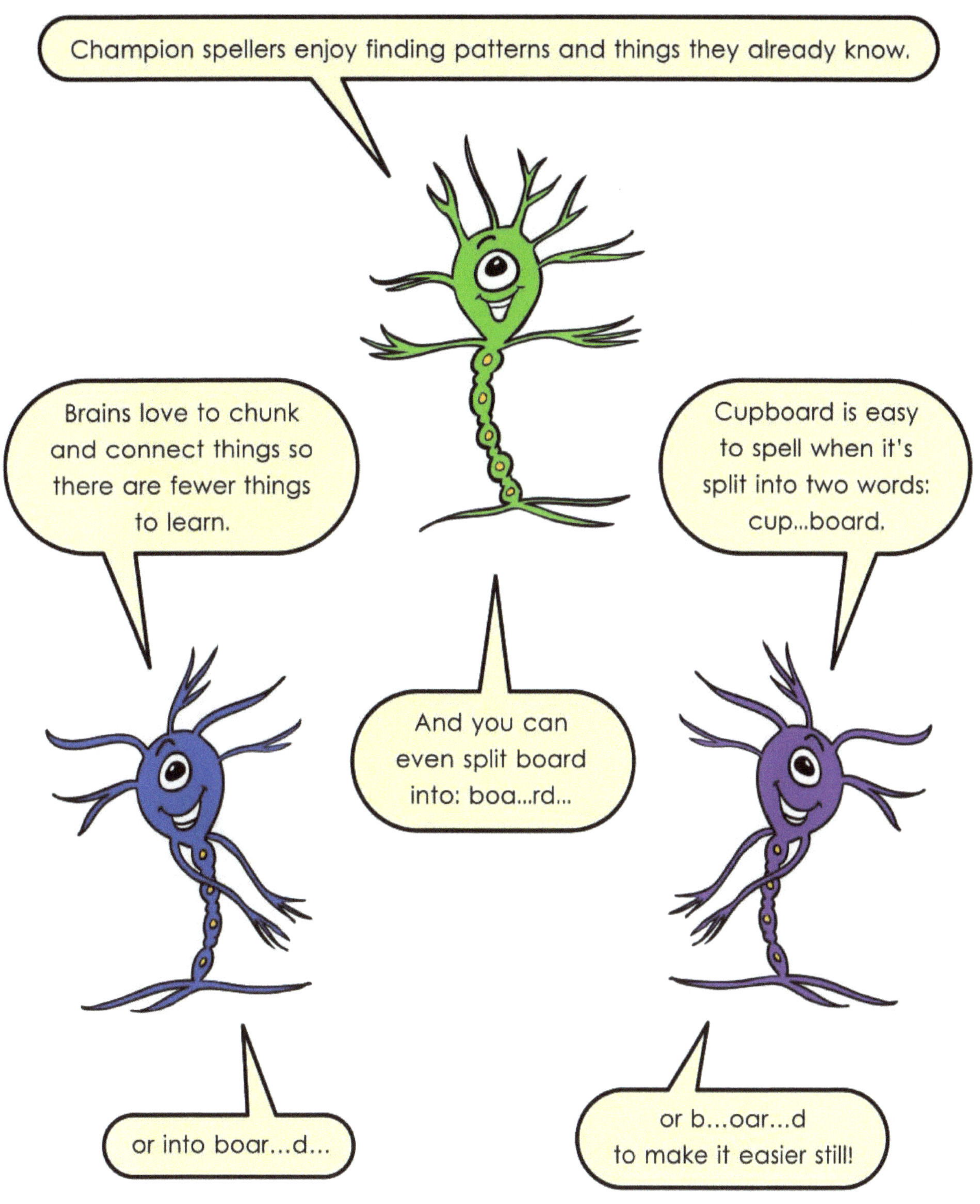

Champion spellers enjoy finding patterns and things they already know.
Brains love to chunk and connect things so there are fewer things to learn.
Cupboard is easy to spell when it's split into two words: cup...board.
And you can even split board into: boa...rd...
or into boar...d...
or b...oar...d to make it easier still!

#  ⭐ Quiz ⭐

Write the letter **T** for true or **F** for false.

Champion spellers:

...... **see words in their minds.**

...... **look for things they already know.**

...... **look at all the letters.**

...... **do spelling tests using a banana instead of a pen.**

...... **make it easy by splitting words into chunks.**

...... **see words in words to make it even easier.**

...... **always stand on their heads to do spelling tests.**

Check your answers with those at the back of the book.

All correct? Fantastic! You've learned the Spelling Champions' magic tricks! You will soon find spellings as easy as they do.

**Colour in the next bit of Holly's picture on page 10.**

# Words in Words game

How many words can you see hiding in these words? People's names
don't count but plurals do. Here are some clues:
- two of these words have one word hiding in them,
- one word has two,
- one word has four,
- the others have three:

Truth  _______________________________________________

Believe  _____________________________________________

Demure  _____________________________________________

Crimson  _____________________________________________

Carpet  ______________________________________________

Rummage  ____________________________________________

These have even more words hiding in them:

Fortunate  ___________________________________________

Palpitate  ___________________________________________

Leather  _____________________________________________

How many words can you find in this last one?

Fundamentalist  ______________________________________

_______________________________________________________

Check your answers with those at the back of the book. All correct? Great!
**Colour in the next bit of Holly's picture.**

# The Lemon Game

Decide who will go first.
Tell the person whose go it is to close their eyes.

Give them these instructions:

- **Imagine you're looking at a lemon.**
- **What colour is it? What does its skin look like?**

- **Imagine you're picking it up.**
- **What does it feel like?**

- **Imagine you're lifting it up to your nose. Can you smell it?**

- **Imagine you're putting it on a chopping board.**
- **Imagine picking up a sharp knife (be careful!) with your other hand.**

- **Imagine you're cutting the lemon very carefully into two halves.**
- **Put the knife down.**

- **Imagine you're picking up one half of the lemon. Look carefully at**
- **it. How many pips can you see? Is there juice oozing out onto your**
- **fingers?**

- **Now put it into your mouth and bite into it.**

If the other person has done this properly they will pull the most disgusting face when they think of biting the lemon.

The winner is the one who pulls the most horrible face (you'll have to ask another friend to decide who wins).

**Colour in the next bit of Holly and her shopping (Page 10) when you've played this game.**

Disgusting variation:
Imagine cutting and biting into an onion or garlic!

Bramble teaches the dogs how to see things in their minds.
Seeing words in your mind is easy.
You can see pictures in your mind can't you?
No! We can't.
Do you have dreams at night?
Yes.
So you can see pictures in your mind.
Suppose so.
What colour is your kennel?

It's light brown. My name is on a red name plate.
Oh no, it isn't. It's grey.
HOLLY
CHARLIE
You're wrong. It's light brown like mine but your name plate's a different colour.
Have another go Holly. You know you can see pictures in your mind.
Oh! So cool! It's light brown and I can see my name on a blue name plate.
Excellent! You can see pictures and words in your minds! You'll soon be spelling Champions!
HOLLY
CHARLIE

#  Quiz

Seeing pictures and pictures of words in your mind.

To colour in more of Holly's picture, answer Yes or No to the questions below:

Do you dream at night?                                  **Yes/No**

Do you see pictures in your dreams?                     **Yes/No**

So your brain knows how to see pictures?                **Yes/No**

Are words a type of picture?                            **Yes/No**

So your brain can see pictures of words?                **Yes/No**

When you've answered **Yes** to all these questions you are well on the way of becoming a champion speller!
**Colour in the next bit of Holly's picture on page 10**.

If you have answered **No** – think and do the quiz again! Words are just a type of picture that everyone can see in their minds. Even if you don't realise it, you are already doing it.

Some people find it easier to see a word

in their mind's eye by **writing it in the air**.

# Writing your name in the air

Lift up your elbow so your hand is at a comfortable
distance away from your face and level with your eyes.
Your magic finger pen points away from your face into the air.



Imagine you're writing your name in the air.
Whisper your name as you're writing it.

Spell your name by reading out all
the letters starting with the first letter.



Now spell your name backwards
by starting with the very last letter.

Holly has been mixing up 'their' and 'there' so Bramble helps her remember which one to use.

Basically one is about people and the other is about a place.

How do I know which one to use?

Their means 'belonging to people'.
So think of i as a funny person.

There is a place so picture the r as a sign post with e dangling off it.

I can see here inside there. Here is a place – so there and where must be places too.

Brilliant! Your way is best for you. There's a word hidden inside their, too... heir is a person. So think of the Queen and Prince Philip, their heir is Prince Charles.

Doh! Didn't know what 'heir' meant and that it sounded like 'air'.

Never mind! You'll soon be champion spellers.

Cool! I like the signpost idea best... but my i is going to be a chewy stick we've chewed a bit. So you'll know it's their chewy stick – not yours.

That's really clever, Holly. Everyone's different and has different ways of remembering things. Choose what works for you.

# Put on your Spelling Head to get into ⭐ your very own Spelling Space ⭐

Now you know all the Spelling Champions tricks, it's time to put on your Spelling Head and get into your very own, very special Spelling Space.

Getting into your own Spelling Space will help **you** to do **spellings brilliantly**.

Olympic Athletes get 'into the zone' to be able to do their very best and win medals. Your Spelling Space is same sort of thing – your zone for learning spellings.

Some Olympic athletes use Heartmath® to get into the zone. They have to breathe before a competition and so they just breathe in this special way, with their eyes open. So use the Olympic champions' way to get into your own zone for spellings: your own Spelling Space.

Follow these three easy steps:

**1**

Breathe a little bit slower and deeper than usual, whatever is comfortable for you.

This gives your Brian Cells more oxygen for extra energy.

and

helps them to join up with each other

and

makes it easier for **you** to be better at thinking and remembering.

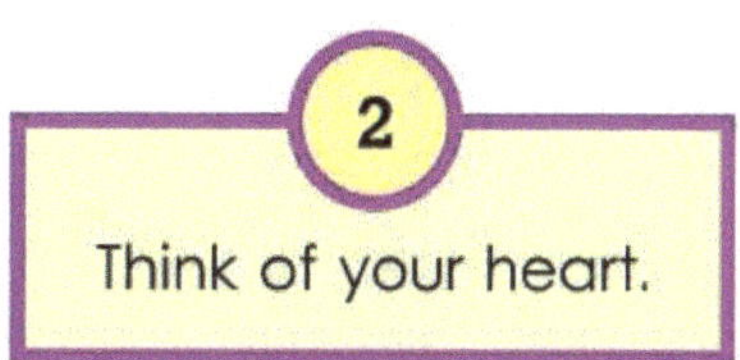


Most people find it easier to think of their heart when they use these three steps:

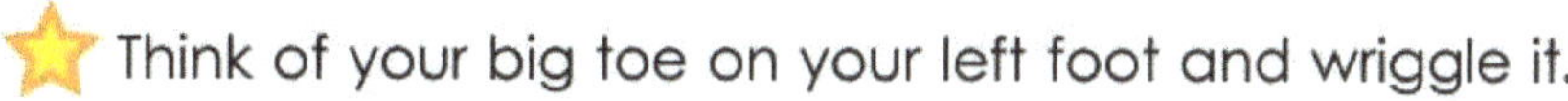 Think of your big toe on your left foot and wriggle it.

Think of your little finger on your right hand and wriggle it.

Think of your heart. You can put your hands where your heart is, if this helps.

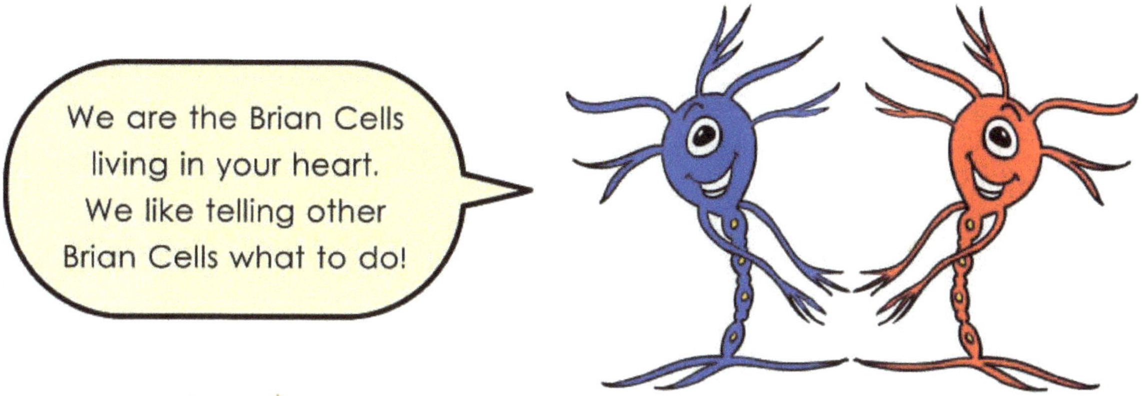

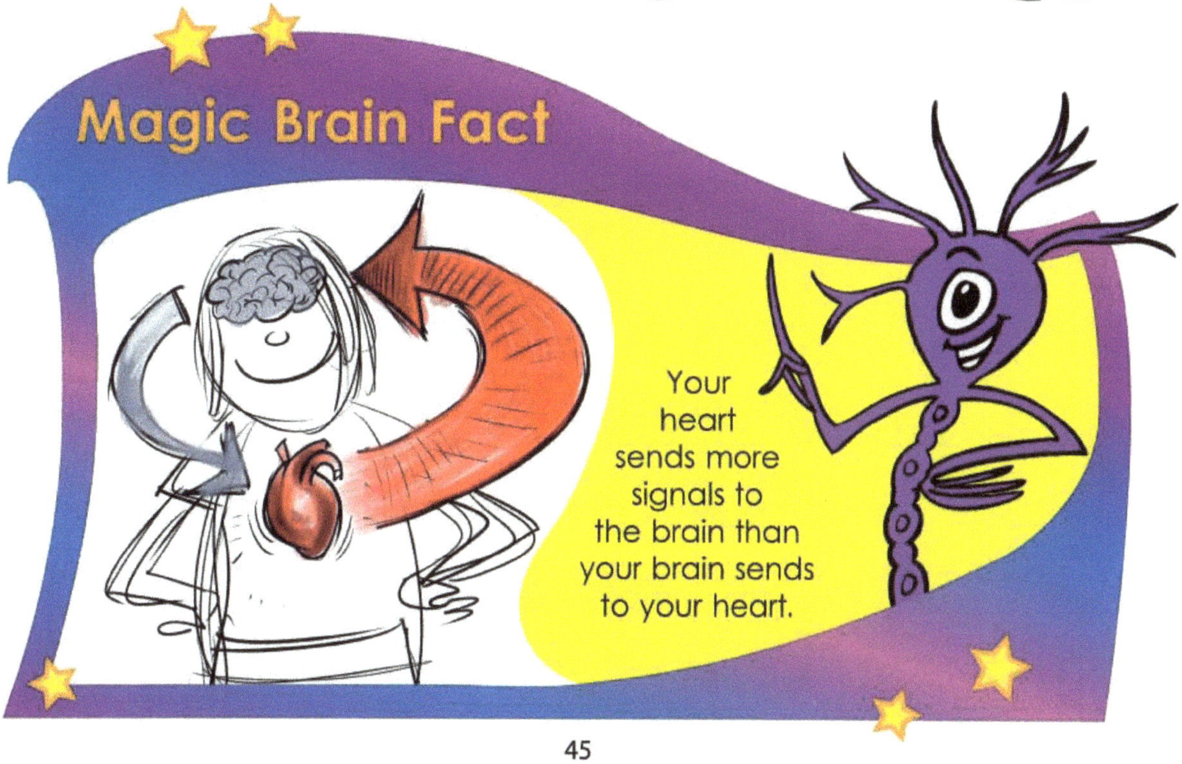

## Magic Brain Fact

Think of something that makes you feel absolutely wonderful.

**Either...**
...something you've done really well:

- A brilliant spelling test OR
- A fantastic sums test OR
- Winning a race OR
- Scoring that goal OR

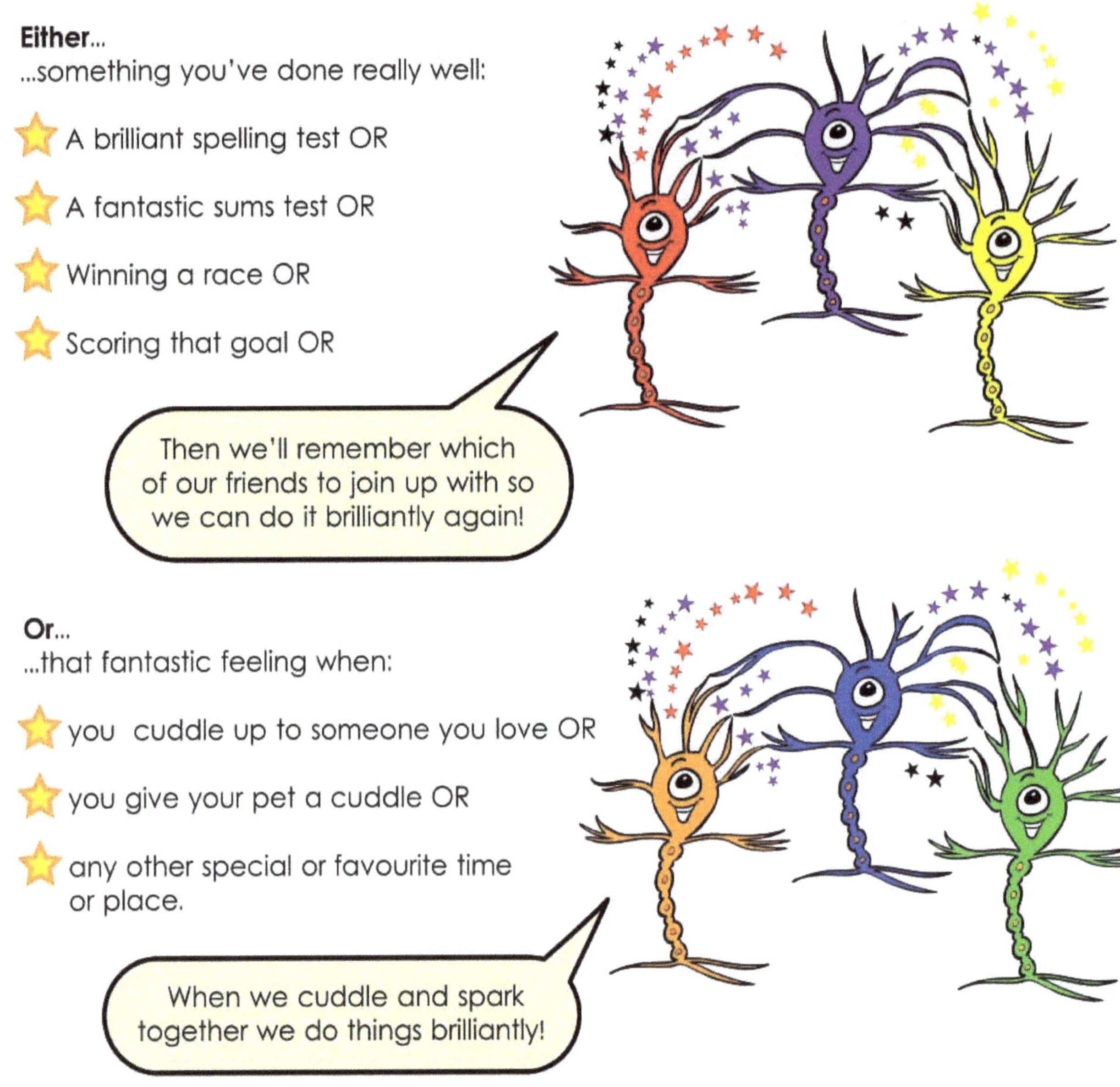


**Or...**
...that fantastic feeling when:

- you  cuddle up to someone you love OR
- you give your pet a cuddle OR
- any other special or favourite time or place.

**See** what you saw... **Hear** what you heard... **Feel** what you felt.

Close your eyes and imagine it's all happening again NOW to make you feel amazing
WOW! I bet you feel absolutely wonderful!

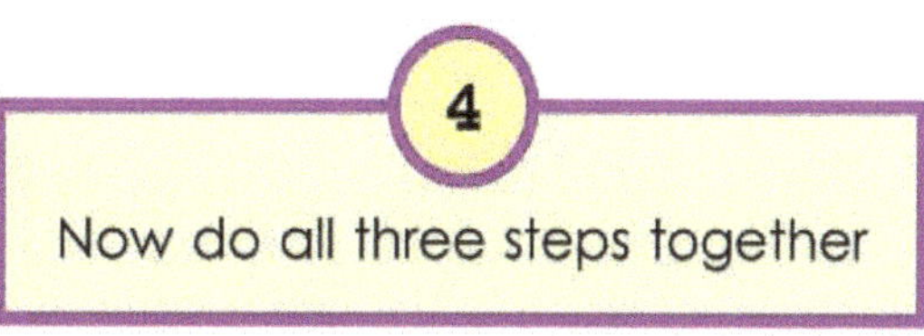


...to help you put on your Spelling Head to get into your Spelling Space.

**1. Breathe a little bit deeper and slower than usual**
This must feel comfortable for you

**2. Think of your heart**
Wriggle your big left toe, little right finger, put your hands over your heart

**3. Think of your wonderful special thing or place.**

**Do this for seven magic breaths before you start learning your spellings.**

Just seven magic breaths instead of your seven normal breaths will help you learn your school spellings brilliantly.

It's amazing how such a little thing can have such a huge effect – especially when you have to breathe anyway!

Heartmath has helped many people to learn things easily and do their personal best in sport and school work.

**Now you know how to get into your Spelling Space, colour in the next bit of Holly's picture on page 10.**

peace

piece

I could do with a tasty piece of pie. Is it nearly dinner time, Charlie?

# How to tackle your school spelling list

Now you know all the spelling champions' tricks you will find this easy.
Start by putting on your Spelling Head to get you into your Spelling Space then:

## Look,

⭐ at every single letter...
especially double letters, tricky letters or silent letters

⭐ for words in words, small chunks or something you already know.

## Say,

⭐ Say it slowly and carefully.

## Write in the air,

⭐ If you prefer do 'click! click! click!'

## Spell it out forwards

## Spell it out backwards

## Now you are there!

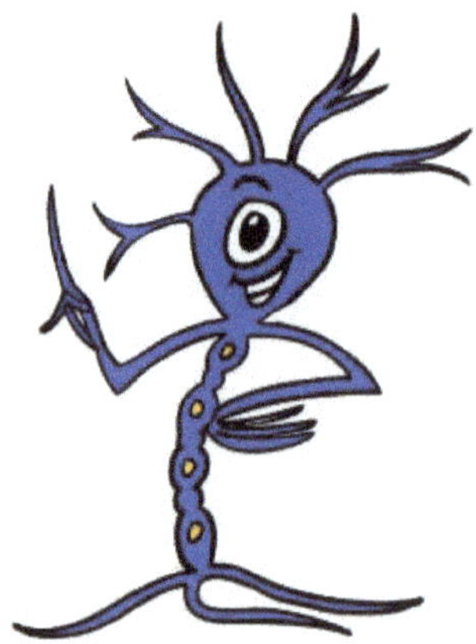

You should have got this spelling by now so all you need to do is to write it on paper and check that **every single letter is correct**.

**If it's right**, start learning the next word.

**If there's any bit wrong**, learn this bit as a separate word (using all the steps above). When you get this bit right learn the whole word again.

When you've learned three spellings, check that you can remember them all by writing them down. Go through all the steps above if you've made any mistakes. Then learn some more!

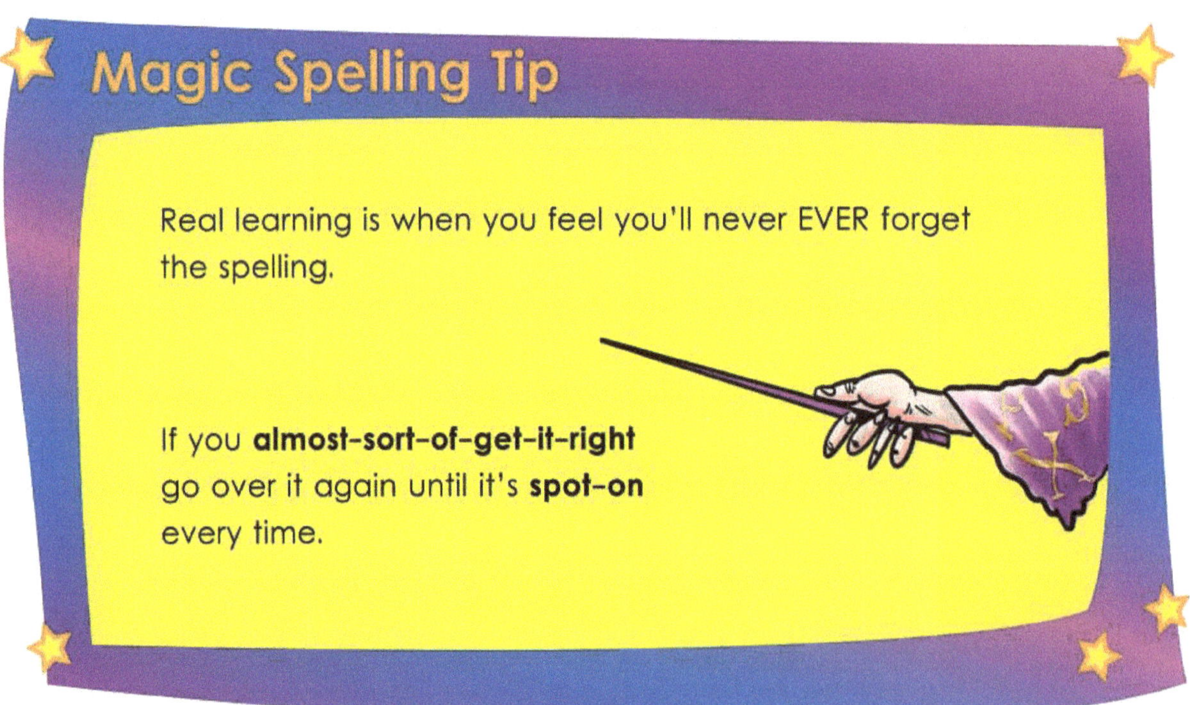

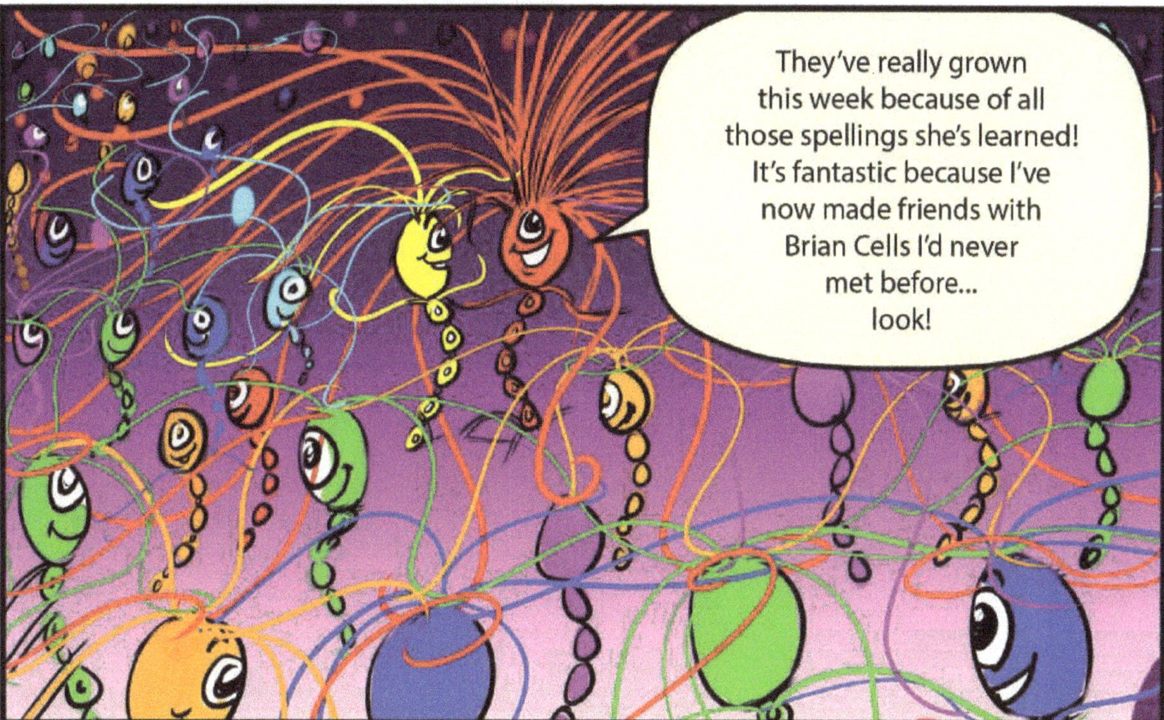


Whenever you learn something new, your Brian Cells' dendrites, or dends, will get longer and thicker so they can join up with more Brian Cells and have a party.

# Brains need to forget things

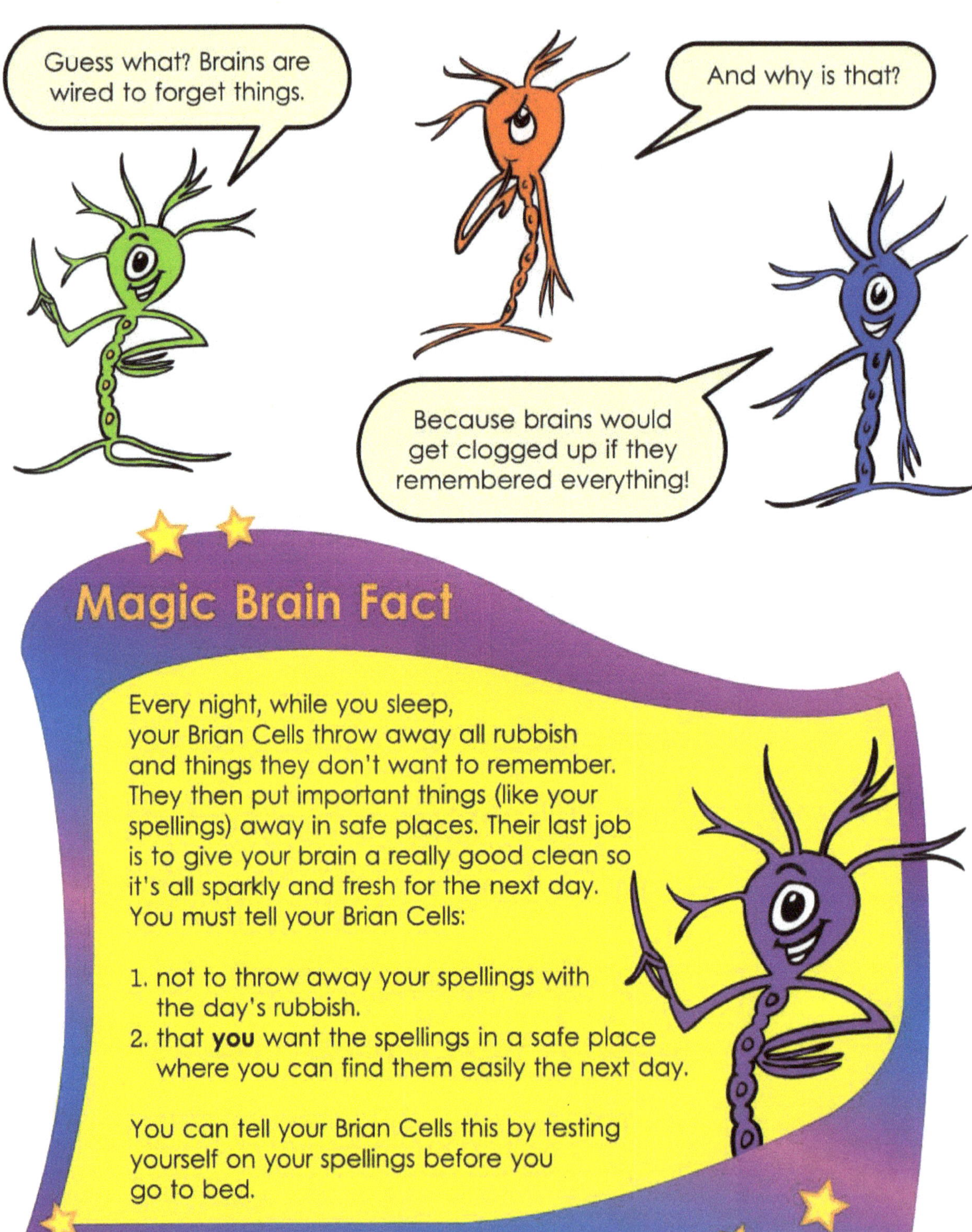



## Magic Brain Fact

Every night, while you sleep, your Brian Cells throw away all rubbish and things they don't want to remember. They then put important things (like your spellings) away in safe places. Their last job is to give your brain a really good clean so it's all sparkly and fresh for the next day. You must tell your Brian Cells:

1. not to throw away your spellings with the day's rubbish.
2. that **you** want the spellings in a safe place where you can find them easily the next day.

You can tell your Brian Cells this by testing yourself on your spellings before you go to bed.

# Magic Spelling Tip

Start learning your spellings as soon as your teacher gives them to you: don't wait until the night before the test.

Learn them the first two nights.
Then you have the rest of the week to quickly revise them every night (especially those harder ones) to make sure your Brian Cells keep them in a safe place. Don't let those Brian Cells throw any of those spellings away with the day's rubbish when they do their nightly cleaning job.

Excellent!
You've done really well to reach the end of this book.
Colour in the last bit of Holly's picture to make her a very happy waggy tailed dog!
Everything she wanted from the internet has now arrived thanks to you because you have helped her with her spellings.

Furthermore, you are now poised to be a champion speller yourself because you have learned how to put the
spell
in
spellings!

# About the author, illustrator and graphic designer

## Dr Sue Whiting - the author

Dr Sue Whiting, Memory Grand Master and five times (1994 -1998) Women's World Memory Champion, has more than 20 years' experience in the field of memory at all levels. She has lectured and coached a wide range of clients in practical memory techniques and strategies to solve their memory and learning problems. A qualified Chartered Accountant and Chartered Tax Adviser (though no longer practising), Sue now works as a writer, speaker, coach and independent memory consultant.

Sue became interested in how the memory works soon after her children arrived.  A career break enabled her to develop her interest, become a Memory Grand Master and the Women's World Memory champion. In doing so, Sue realised that all the hard study that she had done to pass her university and professional exams could have been much more effective.  After experimenting and doing intensive training to develop her visual memory, she smashed the World Record in the Random Images discipline in the 1995 World Memory Championships. This convinced her that the brain is continually changing from day to day and that it is possible to train one's visual memory at any age.

Sue spearheaded the first ever UK schools' memory championships when she devised and wrote all the material and training packs for the 2007/2008 Junior Memory Challenge.  Her work extended to conducting pre-competition trials as well as being arbiter for the final. Year 4 children from sixty primary schools participated and the positive feedback received showed the tremendous demand there was for teaching children how to use their memories effectively.

Sue has spoken in primary schools (even teaching some of the teachers!) and also conducted the popular Wizard of Spells lectures held at the Science Museum in August 2012. Her ideas for the children's Wizard of Spells series of books were developed from these experiences.

She was inspired to become an NLP Practitioner once she discovered the NLP claim that the only way of spelling words in English reliably was by using your mind's eye. Sue had already intuited this herself and so was delighted to find an organisation that believed in the same methodology.

Sue trained as a Heartmath Trainer and coach as soon as she realised how powerful the system was after she had experimented in using it after an introductory day. The technique exceeded all her expectations in its ability to transform stress and to help people to reach an optimal state of mind. With Sue's scientific background (the Dr refers to D. Phil in Astrophysics from Oxford University) she is fascinated by the science behind Heartmath. She believes that the deceptively simple breathing exercise should be introduced in all schools to help children from a young age to control their stress levels and achieve their best.

## Rick Coleman

Rick Coleman has been working as a full time caricaturist and cartoonist for 20 years in the studio and on-the-spot at corporate events. His studio work involves private and commercial commissions of caricatures from photos and commissions for magazines and newspapers. Major clients include the Armed Forces and he has established himself as one of the leading artists producing Officers' Mess Caricature Paintings There are now over 150 of his paintings, of up to sixty people in the largest, hanging in Officers' Messes around the world.

Rick was the gag cartoonist for Sport First newspaper for two years with 'Rick's Sporting View'. He has been the cartoonist for Quest magazine since 1999. He had caricatures commissioned by 'This Morning' show for the last series of 'I'm a Celebrity Get Me Out of Here' and has been producing comic strip art for the Talk Sport radio advertising campaign. His work regularly appears in ITN and Channel 4 News items. He recently appeared as a guest on the Alan Titchmarsh show.
When working on-the-spot, either traditionally or digitally, Rick's style is funny and complimentary, making him a big favourite at weddings and other celebrations. He likes to create a whole picture portraying a full body caricature usually involving a hobby, pastime or themed to the particular event. His live work takes him to all types of events across the country and abroad, including exhibitions, grand prix, conferences, weddings, bar and bat mitzvahs, product launches and golf days. This is the first time Rick has produced illustrations for a children's book.


## Deakin Brook

Deakin Brook, who did all the graphic design, is already a published illustrator having created the illustrations for the captivating books, Is That My Watson and Is that My Holmes, written by Andrew Murray.

After graduating from Camberwell College of Art and Design, Deakin works full time as a graphic designer. He has the skill to be able to draw together all components, adding his own creative ideas where necessary, so as to produce imaginative and creative designs from many different elements.